Kaleidoscope

Russ Towne

© 2016 Russ Towne
Kaleidoscope
First Edition, May 2016

Russ Towne Publishing
Campbell, CA

Editing: Shayla Eaton, CuriouserEditing.com
Cover design: Joleene Naylor, JoleeneNaylor.com
Layout: Gail Nelson, e-book-design.com

Illustration: Christina Cartwright, www.DigitellDesign.com

ISBN 978-0-692-72351-7

Dedication

To Mitch Slomiak, a wise man, but far
more importantly to me, a kind one.
I count his friendship among my greatest blessings.

Acknowledgments

Thank you to the following the people whose excellent work enhanced this creation:

Shayla Eaton of Curiouser Editing

Gail Nelson of eBook Design for layouts of this book for hardcover, softcover, and eBook formats

Joleene Naylor for cover design

Thank you also to the following folks for taking the time to provide ideas and feedback about various aspects of this book:

Annette Rochelle Aben
Jan Beek
Penny Howe
Beth Kennedy
Ute Lark
P. E. Read
Karen Stanford

Contents

A Bad Day's Brewin'

When I woke up

Key sites were down

Spent all mornin'

On work-arounds

Cut a toe on a tack

I didn't see on the floor

Jumped and banged my head

On the edge of a door

Bathroom flooded

Sewer's blocked

I'm even wearin'

Mismatched socks

Coffee pot's empty

It's plain to see

A bad day's brewin'

It's burnin' me

All this stuff

Is pilin' on

Everything I touch

Is turnin' out wrong
But today isn't going
To get me down
It may take awhile
But I'll bring it around
Time will tell
I am right
I'll make it a great day
If it takes all night!

A Bad Habit

I know how bad it can be
To have big expectations.
Too often the reality
Brings sadness and irritation.

A Battle Raged

A battle raged outside my window

I was witness to the awesome show

Between the clouds, wind, rain, and sun

They fought and fought not to be outdone

Clouds and wind were fickle allies

In the ever-changing skies

First fought off the sun and helped the rain

Then they changed sides yet again

But silence came to the gray and blue

A rainbow had declared a truce

But no one really settled down

They just prepared for another round

Without a doubt, they all knew

The battle would soon begin anew.

A Better Man

When I've felt lonely
I've often found
It's not the quantity
Of those around
It's the quality
I understand
That helped me be
A better man.

A Better Measure

When one falls down again and again
Getting back up is an important start
But it's what one does when they do
That's a better measure of their heart!

Abyss

I know too well

What it's like

To linger

On the jagged edge

Of a deep and dark abyss.

Felt its pull.

Heard its siren's song.

"Give up! Give in!

End your pain and shame.

No need to suffer anymore."

But even during my darkest days

When hope was but a memory

I knew even then

The abyss would lose.

That false friend

Has no chance

Against a tool I use.

It renews my hope,

Helps me to endure

When all seems lost.

I make a list of

All I'm grateful for.

I smile as the list grows long.

The abyss loses its allure.

When I'm feeling down,

Counting blessings

Is the cure.

Aglow

Aglow in gratitude

Thankful for . . .

Well, everything

Enjoying today

And wondering

What blessings

And miracles

Tomorrow

May bring

A Smarter Start

To deal with insults,
A much smarter start
Instead of thicker skin
Is a stronger heart.

A Beautiful Blessing

What a beautiful blessing
That each sunset's delight
Brings the glorious birth
Of another new night!

A Beautiful Choice

I saw a beautiful bloom in the garden today,
So stunning it took my breath away.
I was tempted to snip and bring it indoors
Just so I could enjoy it more.
But it was so pretty
It seemed a pity
To deprive the world
Of its petals unfurled.
I lingered awhile,
For it made me smile,
Then carried a memory
But no flower inside with me.

Adversity and Me

I can choose to let adversity
Weaken or strengthen me
The choice is mine
Every time

A Life So True

They say war is hell and it's true
But even in war, there are rules
You tend to know friend from foe
But in gossiping anything goes.
No one is safe from whispered words
Spoken when one's back is turned.
Power comes from dirt that's shared
Whether true or not, few seem to care.
Stab friends in the back with a smile
Pretend to like them all the while
The only defense it seems to me
Against this cruel conspiracy
Is to live a life so true
No one believes gossip 'bout you.

All the Way

Going all the way sexually

Heck, that's the easy part

Compared to

What it takes

To follow through

In matters of the heart

A Million Miles from Anywhere

I'm a million miles from anywhere
Run hard all my life
Got no home, money, or family
No love, girlfriend, or wife.
Every direction I have chosen
Just moved me farther away
From finding love and happiness
Or a welcoming place to stay.
Wanting to be somewhere
No clue where that may be
I'm a million miles from anywhere
And even farther away from me.

A Perfect Time

When my life becomes too rushed
I've learned that's a perfect time
To heed the whispers of my heart
And ignore my harried mind.

A Tough Teacher

When I begin to believe
I've got life licked
It shows me in many ways
I'm far from mastering it.

Back in the Flow

"When I make plans, life often intrudes."
I've come to believe that's just an excuse.
I find plenty of time to get back in the flow
When I focus on things that help me grow.

Beautifiers

*Cheerfulness and contentment are great beautifiers
and are famous preservers of youthful looks.*

—Charles Dickens

I agree they are indeed
Those attributes and attitudes
Along with kindness and gratitude
Beautify lives and worlds.

Beyond My Blindness

When I focus on things that help me grow

I find all kinds of time to get back in the flow.

When I focus on things that make me laugh

That's when I know I'm on the right path.

When I focus on things that make me feel

I find whole new ways to help me heal.

When I focus on things like love and kindness

I begin to see beyond my blindness.

Big Hawk and Little Bird

I stopped to watch a majestic hawk circle a tree
Which stood fifty feet in front of me
Then something tiny caught my eye
A flash of feathers streaked through the sky.
His wings beat so fast they blurred
As he flew into the larger bird
That was at least four times the size
Of that brave and frantic little guy.
The little bird it was clear to me
Was trying to protect his family.
His mate and chicks were in a nearby nest
And this little guy would never rest.
He'd never back off or back down
As long as the big hawk was around.
The prey would keep at him all day
Until he chased the predator away.
Failure for the hawk meant he'd be hungry.
But if little bird lost, the cost would be his family.

So little bird never stopped to pause

Despite the other's much larger claws.

Little bird kept swooping back

Never letting up on his attack.

It took awhile but the battle was won

The hawk turned tail and began to run.

Little bird gave it all he could give

He made the hawk miss a meal

So his family could live.

Bliss

In a hammock on a perfect spring day,

A gentle breeze caressing my skin

With the lightest of touches,

In a verdant garden

Of innumerable flowers,

Flaunting their colorful beauty,

Fragrances tantalizing my senses

As I soak it all in.

Breaking Free

My heart aches when I see

Tortured souls in our society

They toil, fret, and scheme

To chase someone else's dream

So desperate in their quest

For material success

They jump through hoops

In all the right ways

To find only heartache

At the end of their days

Put too much faith in physical things

Unaware of the regrets that approach brings

Seeking approval from without

Is not what success is all about

It is when I came to see

How much happier I could be

Doing all the things I love
Not just a job I was tired of
And true success became a fact
When those I loved
Loved me back

Breakthrough

Darkness dominates.

A faint glow appears.

Patient.

Persistent.

Chipping away.

Lightens.

Brightens.

Until only a wisp remains

To hold it back.

Then that too dissolves.

Breakthrough!

Broken Promise

An unopened bud

A leaf left unfurled

A loss of great beauty

To a beckoning world

Withered by fear

From memories and pain

Won't risk rejection

Shame and disdain

Unrealized potential

Hidden deep in a ball

They suffer in silence

A broken promise to all

Kindness can open

Closed buds over time

Heal shattered hearts

And help fearful minds

A bud can be opened

By the love of a friend
Who believes in their dreams
So their spirit can mend
Sometimes it takes
The smallest of sparks
A word to encourage
Those alone in the dark
Nurturing love
Can go a long way
To help beautiful petals
Feel the light of each day
Bask in the glory
Of knowing they dared
Make the world better
By the beauty they shared
Often late bloomers
Are most lovely of all
As their beauty is deeper
From their time in the ball

Changes

It used to be

I'd refer to a calendar

If I wanted to see

What day of the week it was.

Later I didn't think twice

Because I'd see it on

An electronic device.

Sadly, now I know the day

Because of the pills still left

In my medicine tray.

Clouds

Liquid smoke

Ever-changing

Ethereal and ephemeral

Whispering wisps

Bellowing billows

Drifting away

Cocoons and Choices

We emerge from warm cocoons each morning

A new chance to spread wings and fly

What we do in our waking hours

Defines who we are and why

Hide in shadows of fear and shame

Deny the world and ourselves 'til we die

Or share the glorious gifts we're given

All the beauty and love we have inside.

Conflicting Feelings

At times the natural beauty

Of a person or scene

Is so pure and intense

It takes my breath away.

I'm often left

With a feeling

Of profound joy

But other times

I feel deep and lingering sadness.

Knowing that all external beauty

Is fragile and fleeting.

Creation

I was lost
'Til I dared
Look inside
Find myself
Feel my spirit
Hear my heart
Create the life
I needed to live.

Crimson in a Yellow World

The garden in front of our home

Is graced by many rosebushes.

My Beloved

Lovingly

Planted them

Many years ago.

I now nurture them.

Gorgeous yellow blossoms

Explode from a whole row of them,

Vibrantly glowing in the warm sunlight,

Petals quivering with delight,

From caresses of a gentle breeze.

Oddly, in the middle of one of them,

A branch of deep crimson blooms.

The sight is visually jarring

Yet beautiful.

Of all the rosebushes,

My eyes are most drawn to it.

I often feel

Like one

Of the crimson blooms

Among all of the radiant yellow ones.

Not better,

Nor worse,

Not more beautiful,

Nor less,

Just different,

Yet the same.

Dappled Shadows

Dappled shadows on our path
Filtered light through verdant leaves
Treading softly hear the whispers
Ancient dance of wind and trees.

(Genesis: When I wondered if I had any poetry inside me as a fifty-something-year-old man, this is the first poem I wrote. It holds a special place in my heart and started when the phrase "Dappled shadows" came into my head and would not leave until I created something with it. It was once called "The Dance," but I wrote a different poem that I thought better fit the later piece so I've gone back to using "Dappled Shadows" for the title of this piece.)

Dark Beauties

Delightful tree silhouettes

Framed by dusk-dimmed skies

Your verdant beauty turns to black

Before enchanted eyes

You don't complain about the change

As nightfall draws near

You simply use the light that's left

To make your silhouettes appear

Dear Friend

When you're feeling low

The world doesn't care, it seems,

Your bucket list's too rusty

To hold all your dreams

You've got a friend

Who always believes in you

One who'd like to ease your mind

Of all the cares you're going through

Your fears, sadness, tears, and dreams

They are all safe with me

May you soon share my faith

That your dreams will become reality

I believe in your greatness

All your goodness too

The gifts you have for the world

Most of all, I believe in you

Devil's Dance

Two armies were sent to war

Just to settle a score

By fools with crowns on their heads

And soon ten thousand men were dead.

In the middle of the fight

The bravest young knight

Raged, "Life has no chance

In this Devil's Dance!

Only Death wins an unjust war!"

He flung his weapons down,

On the killing ground,

Uncurled his fist

And took a great risk

Extending his bloody hand.

Would his foe understand?

The other man knew

He could cut him in two,

But sheathed the sword he bore.

He would fight more.

That's the moment when

Five thousand young men

Chose peace that day

And walked away.

Disconnected

When I've said or done some things

That were unpleasant or unkind

I'd disconnected from my heart

And listened to my mind.

Dream-Kiss

Asleep in our bed

So soft and warm.

A gentle touch

On my shoulder

Tells me she's there.

My head slightly lifts,

Sleepy eyes barely open.

She kisses my lips,

Whispers, "I love you"

Then is gone.

(Genesis: I work from home and have no commute, so My Beloved often leaves for work before I rise in the morning. That leads to this morning ritual that I love.)

Enchanted

(song)

Some folks say there's too much silence.

When they're out in the country

If only they could hear

All the sounds that inspire me.

Sunrise brings out the birds

As they begin their own songs,

Except the mockingbird who knows them all

And simply sings along.

Each drop of rain from the storm

Makes a melody

And the voices of a waterfall

Sing in harmony.

The leaves on each tree

Sway to every tune

When darkness falls, the coyotes howl

Their love song to the moon.

They all come together in a wondrous way

To sing and play for me.

I'm enchanted by the forest choir

And nature's symphony

With every note of music

Each whisper of the wind

When I'm away from the country.

I can't wait to go back again

Because nature comes together in a wondrous way

To sing and play for me.

I'm enchanted by the forest choir

And nature's symphony.

(Genesis: This poem became the lyrics of a song titled "Nature's Symphony" that I co-wrote with Kevin Harris. It can be found on Amazon, Spotify, and YouTube.)

Eternity

Our joyous
Cries of passion
Pierced the night.
Love-filled whispers
Caressed delighted ears.
Pleasures promised
And delivered
Soon replaced by
Pain and tears.
Endless silence
And tortured memories
Crushed this once-proud man
And brought me to my knees.
My whole being
Aches for you
My ravaged soul
Laid bare.
The depth of pain
Only rivaled

By the depth of love

We shared.

Even asleep

I still feel

Desire's raging flames.

I jolt awake

Bathed in sweat

Calling out your name.

My flood of tears

Has no chance to quench

The thirst of my desire

While bottomless wells

Of memories

Feed this all-consuming fire.

How do I tell

My trembling hands

And longing lips

Of everything they'll miss?

They'll never again

Caress your skin

Or share your

Breathless kiss.

Our joyous love

That burned so hot

Consumes all thoughts

And memories.

Not long ago

You left my life

When life left you

But to me

It's an eternity.

Ever Since

"What is your most important job of being a wife?"
"To protect his heart," she said to fifty men that day.
"My most important job is to never break his heart."
Her replies to all those guys took my breath away.
My eyes overflowed with pride and love
As the men learned what I already knew.
I've been one of the luckiest guys alive
Since the day she said "I do."

(Genesis: The story in this poem actually happened.)

Every Chance I Get

Don't know what tomorrow will bring
Or even how today will end
But I know that of all my blessings
The greatest are my family and friends.
I could live a long life or die right now
So I take every chance I get
To share all my love and gratitude
So I don't live or die with regret.

Facing the Mirrors

Has my courage held up
On my darkest days?
Have I helped those in need
Along the way?
When facing such mirrors
It's clear to see
I've got more work to do
On me.

Fools' War

We young men
On both sides bleed
Because some old fools
Disagreed.

Forgiveness

Forgiveness

Enables

Hearts

To Let

More

Love

In.

Forty Feet above the Sea

I stare from a small wall

Forty feet above the sea

It stands as a lonely sentinel

Protecting the unsuspecting

From an ugly plunge

To a boulder-strewn beach.

The merciless surf

Pounds unyielding jagged rocks.

The latter gives no quarter,

Breaking up the attack.

Forcing even the mightiest waves

To eventually retreat.

Regroup.

Then strike again.

I never tire of experiencing

Such epic battles.

Though it seems the rocks

Win each day,

The waves are patient,

Unrelenting.

It seems only a matter of time,

Eons perhaps,

Before the waves win,

Grind the great boulders

Into tiny grains of sand.

But perhaps instead,

Several centuries from now,

The sea may recede.

Surrendering, at least for a time.

Then the boulders

Will reclaim their brethren

From the briny depths.

I think such thoughts

And wonder at the spectacle

As I stand at a small wall

Forty feet above the sea,

Knowing I will long be dead and gone

Returned to my own ashes and dust

Before the answer

As to which will be the victor

Is revealed.

For You

Some may like what I write

Maybe many or just a few

Regardless of the number

I'll write for those of you who do.

Games

In many games the rule-makers rule.

They aren't fun and are often cruel.

Nothing good comes for those who play.

They're full of regret at the end of the day.

If it's a game I cannot win,

It's a game I'll not be in.

I could break the rules or try to cheat,

But I'd not feel good in the winner's seat.

Rather than complain and remain

Or find someone else to blame,

When I don't like the game I'm in,

I change to one that I can win,

One I love where I'll have fun

From when I start until I'm done,

Where win or lose, I'll still be me

And always have my integrity.

Gold Fever

It only took a single look

At all that glittering gold

Then once again my heart was held

Embraced in its lustrous hold

Gold Fever has struck again

But not for the shiny metal

My fever's for my favorite flower

The poppy with golden petals

When I behold a field of gold

Adorned by dew drops glistening

As it sways in time with a gentle breeze

My heart can't help but sing.

Good News

I just learned something great
That I truly appreciate:
I lose weight
When I create.

Gossip Machines

Gossip Machines feel the need
To tear people down
But it's the cruel act of a coward
If their victims aren't around
When I talk about people
I attempt to follow a rule:
I'll only share things about others
That are kind, helpful, and true.

Greater than Gold

As I sat eating my meal

Alone in my thoughts and cares

I noticed a little girl

Turn her head and briefly stare.

She saw a homeless man with a hopeless look

Who'd been hungry for far too long.

Her eyes grew sad from what she saw

Then she whispered to her mom.

I don't know what she said

As she pointed to him

But when her mom smiled

There was joy in her eyes again.

The girl's hands held coins

She'd counted every penny.

It was her allowance

And she didn't drop any.

She placed her savings on the counter

Ordered a meal for a man in need

Fidgeted a bit as she waited for it

So anxious to do the kind deed.

He looked up in surprise

And when he saw what she held

His eyes moistened a bit

And his heart seemed to melt.

He took her gift and gave his thanks

They smiled, then she walked away.

It's a good bet I'll never forget

The way I felt that day.

My heart grew lighter

For inside I knew

That his spark of life and spirit

Had grown a bit brighter too.

I learned a lot from that little girl

Who was less than nine years old

How a simple act of kindness

Can be a gift that is greater than gold.

(Genesis: The girl in this story is the daughter of a friend who witnessed her doing this kind and generous act. I decided to honor them both by writing this poem.)

Grief's Fire

When nothing I can say
Will ease another's pain,
If I just show up
Again and again,
And stay in grief's fire
Without shrinking away,
It can help them make it
Through to brighter days.

Guilty

"You have the heart of a poet,"
I was told for the longest time
And now I'm no doubt guilty
Of the rhyming crime.

Heart Whispers

For too long I let

Fear's warnings

Shame's berating

And nagging ego

Make me deaf.

I became

A better man

With a richer life

When I learned

To listen

To the whispers

Of my heart.

Highs and Lows

I never

Feel raised up

When I

Put down

Anyone

But feel lifted

When I give

A helping hand

To others.

Home Maintenance

Our lawns need mowing

A cobweb's growing

A gate is sagging

Repairs are lagging

Shelves are dusty

A latch is rusty

A faucet leaks

Our hall floor creaks

Laundry's piled on the floor

A broken knob is on a door

Our housekeeping is far from kept

But our home's well maintained in some respects

The work we do around our house

Is less on things and more on ourselves

Love and laughter are brightly shined

And we focus on being kind

We don't skimp on telling the truth

But for lies we have no use

Ego corrodes so we remove it fast

That's how we make relationships last

Our home's foundation is built on trust

With big strong beams that'll never rust

Our home is warmed with love all night

And lit all day with love's bright light

Our joy and fun have a brilliant gleam

Trust and faith has a polished sheen

Folks would do well to go somewhere else

If they want to visit a clean house

But if love and friendship are what you prefer

That kind of maintenance we don't defer

So come in, friends, enjoy your stay

May you feel welcome every day.

How?

After thirty-seven years
How slow must I be
That when I'm out with her
She can still trick me?
She says all she needs
Is one thing from a store
But eight hours later
She's bought forty from four!

How You Know

Words that form in my head
Don't do justice to how I feel
But when I speak from my heart
You know my love is real.

If Only...

"If only..." he said
'til the day he died
Let regrets drown
His dreams inside
Paralyzed in the present
By mistakes of the past
Gave up on living
Until dying at last
Few words are so cruel
Or have ruined more lives
They corrode the spirit
And cut like knives
Two little words
But oh, the cost
In dreams shattered
And lives lost
Don't suffer the fate
Of broken-winged birds
Time to break free
From those two little words

I Had Many Plans

They say man plans and the gods laugh

Well, that was certainly true for me.

Most of my dreams and schemes fell through

Though not the love from friends and family.

When my plots and plans crashed down

I never would have believed

It would lead to a life much sweeter

Than I ever could have conceived.

Inside

Too many boxes sit on a shelf

Locked tight by fear and pride

It's not too late to open up

Share all the beauty trapped inside.

In That Instant

Two lonely strangers on opposite walls
Of a room full of partying people
Each wondering how soon they could go
Without being rude,
And why they'd come at all.
Then they saw each other
And in that instant
Both hearts knew
The answer to that question
And that they'd never be lonely again.

(Genesis: I once worked with a lady who, as a young woman, was sitting at a stoplight when a stranger drove up in the lane next to her. Their eyes met. They knew in that instant that they'd met the love of their lives. When I met her, they'd been happily married for about forty years.)

It Depends

Whether the cup is half full or half empty
Of this I have no doubt,
It depends whether I'm pouring something in
Or drinking something out.

It Does

My eyes don't always get it right
My brain is sometimes wrong
So now I trust my heart more than mind or sight
Because when I don't know the answers
To life's toughest questions
It does.

It Helps Me Hear

Too often when I speak
My mind gets in the way,
But when I write it helps me hear
What my heart and soul have to say.

Jonathan? Is That You?

Something blurred by
High in the sky
It was quite an amazing show
As I watched from the shore below
A bright white bird with glowing wings
The fastest seagull I'd ever seen
Soared and plunged again and again
As in a race he had to win
Blazed faster through the air
Than any gull ever dared

I shouted as he flew,

"Jonathan? Is that you?"

He nodded with a wink

Dipped a wing in a blink

I waved to him too

Yelled, "Nice to meet you!"

With a friendly grin, he went on his way

But I'll never forget meeting him that day!

(Genesis: I wrote the poem below as a tribute to the character Jonathan Livingston Seagull from the book of the same name by Richard Bach. I read the book for the first time as a teenager and loved its messages about following my passion, choosing my own way in life, and that it is okay to feel and to be different.)

Joy

Joy comes to me when I hear
The beating of the smallest heart
And pause in respect and reverence,
When I somehow know and honor
Unspoken dreams,
Welcome with open arms
Those who deem themselves invisible,
And when I comfort-hidden pain.

Kindness Connection

It happens every time

I experience

Love in action

Whether it's

Kindness to me

From me

Or to others by others

I feel a connection

To humankind

The spirit within me

And the universe

That makes my heart smile

Fills me with gratitude

To be alive

And part of it all.

Last Dance

They clung tightly
Knowing when they leapt
It would be forever
Flirted with each other for months
Waiting for just the right moment
For the ultimate release
Then it came
In a reckless rush
They simply let go
Gave in to a power
Greater than them
Caught in a swirling
Twirling sensation
Colors flashed
As the world rushed by
Reveling in every motion
In the beauty all around

And in their partner

Felt a freedom

They had never known

Gloriously floating

Then softly touching

The earth and each other

In a long and final embrace.

(Genesis: When I saw two falling leaves swirl around each other as they fell to the ground, they reminded me of two lovers dancing.)

Let Me Help You Cry

The raging storm inside you that you fear
Will drown you in a flood of tears
If you ever let your feelings show
There's nowhere else for it to go.
I know you're brave and I know you're strong
But you've been treading water far too long.
Your dammed-up feelings are pulling you down
And I won't sit here and watch you drown.
The longer you wait, the stronger it grows.
Fight the fear and let your tears flow.
We'll do it together, I'll help you see
No storm can stop you and me.
We'll get through the flood, outlast this storm.
Make it to a shore that's safe and warm.
Let all the sadness and the pain
Fall like rain
From your beautiful eyes.
Let me help you cry.

Russ Towne

Letting Loose

I was in a goofy mood today

Came up with something silly to say

It's fun for me to try to find

Crazy ways to use near-rhymes

Like, "I had a bottle of water

For my trip to Guadalajara."

What's so fun about being serious?

I ask myself when I get curious

Sometimes poets must let loose

Go a little nuts and be obtuse

There's no crime in internal rhyme

Heck, I do it all the time

While alliteration can be overdone

It for me is lots of fun!

Though this poem won't win for style

I sure hope it makes you smile.

Life Lesson

Life
Is for Learning.
Love
Is the Lesson.

Love in Action

My life changed forever
Became so much better
When I learned kindness and passion
Are both love in action.

Lovers' Wish

For those who seek their soul mate
And for those whose lover is away:
May you soon hold your love so close
That your two hearts beat as one.
May your love grow stronger every hour
And hotter still when each day is done.
May your passion burn so bright
That its glow lights up the skies
And may you both bask in the sight
Of undying love in each other's eyes.

May This Prove True for You

When I thought of all
You're going through
This came to me
And I hope it's true:
The harder
Your pregnancy
The easier
Your labor
And happier
And healthier
Your child
Will be!

(Genesis: When one of my dear daughters-in-law was carrying what we thought was to be our second grandchild, she experienced extreme morning sickness that often lasted all day even with medication, and kept her bedridden. When I thought of what she was going through to bring My Beloved's and my second son's first child and our second grandchild into this world, this came to me. It turns out she was carrying twins and she and the boys are healthy!)

Mirages

It happened without warning
One moment I could see fine
Then my eyeglasses broke
And I felt nearly blind
But my fuzzy vision
Brought into sharp relief
That what happened to my eyes
Can happen to my beliefs
Opinions built on air
Can come crashing to the ground
And sometimes "facts" no longer fit
With biases brought down
Now my eyes once again
See with clarity
With help from new glasses
That are a better fit for me
But what about my false beliefs
When they're shattered on the ground?
And the mirages I had counted on
Are nowhere to be found?

Muse Misery and Ecstasy

Muses can often be
The most horrible teases
Before finally sharing
Something that pleases!

My Company

Used to dread
Being alone
Like a long-lost dog
Far from home
Then one day
I made a plan
To make myself
A better man
No longer lonely
Alone with me
I actually like
My company

My Dream

I dream

Of the blessed day

When humanity awakens

From its terrible nightmare

And works for peace

With as much

Ferocity, tenacity, and heroism

As we've fought our wars.

My Old Friend

(song)

You picked me the moment we met

And you knew right from the start

We were supposed to be together

You ran straight to my arms and into my heart.

I couldn't ask for a more loyal companion

You'd risk your life to save mine.

When I was sick in bed for a week

You stayed right by my side the whole time.

You once ruined our brand-new carpet

When you ate my whole birthday cake.

My wife forgave us because you're cute

Though getting sick is no excuse for the mess you made!

But I'm far from perfect too

I can be cranky for days

When I growl 'n bark and snap at you

You still always love me anyways.

(Bridge)

Your face is growing whiter and your pace is off a step

Let's make the most of whatever time we have left.

(Chorus)

My Old Friend,

Life with you is better, My Old Friend

It's always an adventure I wish would never end,

And I'm glad we have each other, My Old Friend!

So glad we have each other, My Old Friend.

(Genesis: This started as a poem about my dog Duke and turned into a lyric for a song honoring the deep bond of love between many people and their dogs and other pets. The song can be heard on YouTube, Amazon, and Spotify.)

Naturally

All those who love nature
Probably also love their lives
For nature is full of life
And happy lives are full of love.

Need's Answered Call

Love in action is a beautiful sight.
My whole heart smiles
And the world feels right.
Kindness and connection
Make my spirit glow
My joy's so great
Tears overflow.
I feel so grateful
For need's answered call.
I'm blessed to be alive
And part of it all.

No Doubt

I have

No doubt

That it

Is when

I look

Within

That I

Will thrive

Without.

No Need for a Key

I searched for the key to happiness
Sought joy from far and wide
Looked everywhere I knew
But never looked inside
Then one day it came to me
When I stopped to take a rest
How much time I had wasted
In my search for happiness
I knew right then I'd been wrong
In that which I'd supposed
For all the time I'd sought the key
The door was never closed!

Pack Mule

She says, "We don't need a shopping cart
I'll just get an item or two."
So why am I clutching thirty things
When she's only halfway through?

Possibilities

May

Love

Overwhelm

Fears

And

Open

Hearts

To joyous

Possibilities

Rainstorm Moments and Memories

Sitting outside

Near the edge of an overhang

As rain thunders down

Drops splash so close

They mist my face.

Drops of sweet freshness

Mix with fragrance of flowers

Speak to my spirit

Promising life

Growth and abundance.

Raindrops caress

Silky petals

Gifting them

With nature's pearls

Sparkling radiance

Of diamonds.

Flowers seem

Even prouder

Of their elegance

When enhanced

By such adornments.

Two sets of wind chimes

Vie for my attention

With beautiful melodies

Capturing the wind

While being captured by it

One chime passionately proclaims

Of romantic young lovers

The other whispers of

Those who've shared

A lifetime of memories.

For a moment I'm tempted

To stand in the downpour

Reveling

In the physical sensations

It offers.

Memories flow

Of such times.

Staccato taps

On my head and shoulders

The way it caresses

With cold fingers

As it slides down my face

Brings chills to my spine

Whispers ever-so-softly

As it slides from my ears.

My sweet reverie

Is interrupted

As the rain falls no more

But my smile and memories linger.

Right Here

I see you're a survivor and surrender's not your way

I know the courage it can take just to face another day

I know too well how horrible some things in life can be

And the cost of all you've lost so devastatingly

I'll help you find forgiveness for those who did you wrong

So you can purge the pain and hurt that's festered for too long

Poison from a wound so deep it's slowly killing you

I know the symptoms all too well because I've had them too

From all your grief and torment I'll help you find release

For you deserve a life of joy and greater inner peace

I'll hold you tightly in my arms and whisper in your ear,

"You are safe, you are loved, and I'm staying right here."

Salty Paradox

How can something as loud and violent
As powerful pounding waves
Crashing on jagged rocks
Make me feel so calm and peaceful?
Could it be the salt in the sea
Calling to the salt from the sea in me?

Satisfaction

I'm often asked in what I believe
And the goals I'm trying to achieve.
Kindness gives me satisfaction.
In other words, Love in Action.

Russ Towne

See You Soon

What are those big ugly things?
Caterpillars asked about her wings.
She knew they wouldn't understand
It was part of a master plan.
She gave them all a warm goodbye,
"See you soon when you've wings to fly!"

She Loves Fragile Things

She loves fragile things
Stained-glass windows and butterfly wings,
Snowflakes, flowers, and figurines
She's careful with all such things.
But she knew right from the start
To be extra careful with my heart,
Because she wisely understands
My fragile heart is in her hands.
And if she ever broke my heart
It would tear my world apart.

Shine

May your love
Always shine on me.
May I bask in your glow
For eternity.
May I feel your sweet love
Every day
And your healing warmth
In every way.

Silly, Silly Me

He grabbed my hand and yelled, "Come see! Come see!"

And excitedly pointed to our big shade tree.

"Yes, I see; it's a tree," I thoughtlessly said.

With wise young eyes, he shook his head.

"Silly Grandpa, can't you see?

It's not just a tree! It's so much more.

It's a place to play, to build, to climb, to explore.

A secret place to talk and hide

Or to pretend that we're real spies!"

Now it was my turn to shake my head.

"Silly, silly me! Of course!" I said.

"How could I have forgotten?

It is much more than a tree!

The years had blinded these old eyes

To all the things a tree can be.

Thank goodness you were here

To help me to once again see!"

"Grandpa, come see what else I've found!

It's big, light brown, and on the ground."

Slow learner that I am, I said to him:

"It's the box our refrigerator came in."

"Silly Grandpa," he sighed and said, "Can't you see?

It's not just a box; it's anything we want it to be!

A great big castle with a moat

A pirate ship or ranger boat

A fire engine that fights huge fires

Or a monster truck with great big tires.

A real fast car that we can race

Or a rocket ship in outer space.

A screaming jet that we can fly

Or a helicopter up real high

It can even be a submarine

See? It can be anything!"

I then remembered a thing or three

About what a cardboard box can be

I shared ideas that I recalled.

He smiled and said, "Grandpa,

You're not so silly after all!"

Smiles

They warm my heart and spirit

And never go out of style

Like the beaming ones couples wear

Walking together down the aisle

Nearly all are wonderful

But some mean so much more

Such as smiles worn by those you love

When you walk through your front door.

Some come from memories

The first smile on a baby's face

And those shared by parents

When they feel a child's embrace.

Proud but sometimes sad ones

When children have all grown

Packed up and moved out

To build lives of their own.

The kind a surgeon wears
After a long and hard fight
That says they'll pull through
Everything will be all right.
They are so often present
When I travel down memory lane
Think back to favorite scenes
To experience them again.

So Much Better

Ego and pettiness
Add to life's travails.
My world works so much better
When kindness prevails.

Stomach Churners

Of life's many lessons
An important one I've learned
Is to stay away from anyone
Who makes my stomach churn.

Suddenly

Suddenly

You just

Know.

When you hear

The whispers

Of your heart,

Love emerges

From your fertile spirit

Where it waited

Patiently

For your understanding

To beautify and inspire

The world.

Swallowed Alive

My heart aches when I see

Tortured souls in society

Toil, fret, and scheme

Chase mirages as their dreams

So desperate in their quest

Lusting for material success

Addicted to physical things

Blind to what that approach brings

Envy and greed are insidious beasts

Rats in their race are their favorite feast

Slither so softly then quickly ensnare

Those lured by desire and so unaware

Sweet cravings and great pangs

Mask the poison-filled fangs

Miss all the signs of wasted lives

'Til they're alone

In the darkness

Swallowed alive

Sweet Mystery

I've never solved

This sweet mystery:

How could she touch

Me more deeply

Than I'd ever be

Without laying

A finger on me?

The Beauty of Your Spirit

The beauty of your spirit

Radiates all over you

I only wish that you could see

Your beauty as I do

The Change

The daunting gauntlet that was my life
Was full of stress, strain, and strife
Felt only pain and misery
Hope seemed a distant memory
It was even hard to lift my head
Or get myself out of bed
Trouble seemed all around
Chains of fear kept me bound
Trapped deep within my lonely room
Imprisoned in a cramped cocoon
Darkness was both foe and friend
Wondered when my ordeal would end
Sadness seemed to be my fate
Thought all I could do was sit and wait
But waiting proved a waste of time
It didn't change this life of mine
It took some action on my part
A major change inside my heart

Began to fix my attitude

View life through a lens of gratitude

Showed kindness to those in need

Found that included even me

Often stopped to smell the flowers

Put much more joy into each hour

Learned to appreciate all I had

Found lots of reasons to be glad

Followed my passion more each day

What was work now was play

Was amazed at just how fast

My life began to improve at last

Now my life is full of song

My heart held the answers all along

The Cost

I sometimes find

When I hope so hard

In one direction

I miss several blessings

That are happening

In other directions,

And the cost

Of my blindness

Is sometimes greater

Than what I would have gained

If what I'd hoped for

Had happened.

The Curb

Alone again on this cold, dark, curb

Shivering in the rain

Waiting out the endless night

Engulfed by pain and shame

Soaked shoes make dams in the gutter

The stream, like life, rushes by

Indifferent to my existence

Too busy to care why I cry

Rain pounds my hatless head

A mighty sea on a broken shore

Magnifies my grief to the point

I can barely breathe anymore

Every drop an icy needle

Running down my neck to my toes

Mirrored by the tears that fall

In a never-ending flow

A searing string of questions

Taunts my tortured mind

How could this have happened?

How could life be so unkind?

It gave me all I wanted

A dear sweet family

Then ripped the lives of my sweet wife

And two young kids from me

That night a sleepy driver

Who was new to our old town

While looking for a street sign

Ran my family down

Their lives were gone in a heartbeat

While my heart beats on and on

I lost my mind the moment

My cherished ones were gone

I knelt with them in the blood and rain

Hugged them tightly to my side

With all my heart I wished they'd lived

And I was the one who'd died

If only I'd run faster

Might've saved my family

Or seen the danger sooner

Such regrets torture me

How can a heart so crushed

Stay alive so long

When everyone it loved

Is suddenly all gone?

So I'm alone again on this cold, dark, curb

Shivering in the rain

Waiting out the endless night

Engulfed by pain and shame.

(Genesis: Thankfully, no part of the following story is true for me and my family. The genesis of this story is that I wanted to see what backstory I'd create for someone whose life had completely fallen apart and they were sitting on a curb in the dark out in the rain.)

The Deepest Parts of Me

Flowers say

To hummingbirds and bees,

"Come caress

The deepest parts of me.

My perfumed petals

Are open wide.

Please fly to me

And come inside."

The First

She whispered, "I like you."
All the prompting I'd need
As we stood in the shade
Of a towering tree
Both new at this
Feeling kind of shy
Leaned toward each other
Quickly closed our eyes
That warm sunny day
Shared our first kiss
She, only five years old
I was almost six.

The Hunger

I often have a hunger

That engulfs me

At the most

Inopportune times.

It fills me

With a need

Far greater

Than mere desire

And can only

Be sated

When I stop

Doing all else

To focus

Exclusively

On putting to words

Feelings and ideas

Gushing

From the depths

Of my heart and spirit,

And offer them

With love

To the world.

The Kind of Dad I Had

As I sat there beside his bed

"I wish I'd been a better dad," he said.

"There are big things I wanted to do

To make your life much better for you

Now my time on earth is nearly done

And I haven't done a single one

The things I did were always small

I barely helped you out at all

I reached to touch his ancient hand

Had to help him understand

"Dad, how do I make you see?

What was small to you was huge to me

When I was weak, you helped me get strong

Always forgave me when I was wrong

When I felt unsafe, you gave me protection

When I got off course, you helped me change direction

When I felt alone, you were there for me

I know in my heart you'll always be

When I got hungry, you kept me fed

When I couldn't walk, you carried me to bed

When I fell down, you lifted me up

When I was thirsty, you filled my cup

When all was bleak, you gave me hope

You got me through when I couldn't cope

When I nearly died, you stayed all night

When it got too dark, you gave me light

I learned so much from watching you

Important things a man should do

You were there no matter what

That's the kind of dad I've got

I'm so blessed and very glad

To have had the kind of dad I've had."

When his eyes closed for the last time

His smile helped to ease my mind

He showed me in his own way

He understood what I'd tried to say

The Kind of Friend I Want to Be

One day I found I had false friends

It broke my heart and I blamed them

But blaming those I couldn't count on

Taught me nothing and I was wrong

I had the friends I deserved

For true friends I'd be better served

To change myself and become one

To learn to do what must be done

Train my eyes to clearly see

What their eyes are telling me

All the things so hard to say

Keep listening 'til they find a way

To share their pain, grief, and fears,

Hear with my heart, not just my ears

Give a hug when they need one

When they're defeated and when they've won

Stand with them in life's hottest fires

Help them achieve what they desire

Then speak my truth while being kind

So they'll know what's on my mind

Share my passions, fears, and dreams,

My best-laid plans and crazy schemes

I do these things for them and me

To be the friend I want to be

I now have friends both tried and true

Who appreciate the things I do

They're there for me and me for them

My life is brighter with true friends

The Open Window

I just opened a window.

In the space of a heartbeat

Magic happened.

My senses are aroused

By sumptuous melodies

Of songbirds singing so near

It seems they've flown into my office

To share their gifts with me.

The scent of rain and flowers

Meld into potent

Olfactory pleasure.

Inches away,

Great multicolored blossoms

Capture my eyes,

Each vibrant petal an invitation

To soak in its beauty

And experience exquisite softness

With a touch.

In this moment,

Life-diminishing concerns disappear.

LIVE! Really LIVE!

That is what I do when I remember

To remove the blinders

Of everyday distractions

From my heart and senses

And truly experience

The wonders all around me.

A profound sense of gratitude,

Joy, connectedness, and peace

Envelops me.

A bit of sadness too,

For letting lack of mindfulness

And a thin pane of glass

Separate me

From all these blessings.

The sadness doesn't last.

How could it when surrounded by

So many miracles?

The Race

Dedicated to Brian and Kristi, parents of our twin baby grandsons

Moving in slow motion

Can hardly think at all

Vision's getting fuzzy

Movements slowing to a crawl

Forgot to leave the porch light on

Can't fit my key in the lock

Tell myself I need more sleep

As I fumble in the dark

It's a slow-motion race

As I stagger through the door

For my head to hit my pillow

Before my face hits the floor.

The Role of a Lifetime

In the movie
Of each of our lives
We can choose to be in
Silent roles and bit parts
Wear masks
Make cameo appearances
Choose to play victims
Rather than risk
Being the heroes
We all can be.
We can follow scripts
Written by others
Or listen
To the whispers
Of our heart.
Poor role choices
Leads to drama and tragedy.

I know this too well

For I've wasted

Much of my life

Playing such roles.

But now there are so many

Great supporting actors

In the movie of my life

That I can't help

But feel like a star.

Russ Towne

The Sweetest Words of All

I've had lots of roles and titles
But of the many things I've been called
"Husband," "Dad," and "Papa"
Are the sweetest of them all!

The Treasure

There are pieces of my spirit
In all that I create
Offers of connectedness
I hope will resonate
May you find what I write
To be loving, kind, and true
Inspiring a deeper delving
Into the treasure that is you
May these bridges of love
Remind all my sisters and brothers
Of the greatness and the goodness
Within yourselves and others

The Wait

Light can be too bright

It can even hurt our eyes

And make us blind

If too much shines at one time

Perhaps truth and wisdom

Are like light's rays

We take in what we can

But the rest must wait for later days

They Know

They see us

Before we see ourselves

Gifts

Talent

Beauty

Dreams

Kindness

Strengths

Creativity

Goodness

Greatness

Everything

That makes

Us worthy

Of Love

Respect

Admiration

They know
Who we are
What we're made of
Inspire us to share
What we have
With the world

They Were

They were

"Committed"

To each other

Mostly

Nearly

Largely

Partially

Almost

Sort of

But one day

They realized

That commitment

Isn't a sometime

Or partial thing

It's all or nothing

And there is beauty

And strength

In commitment

When both

Are ready

Thoughts of You

Seemingly from out of nowhere

Thoughts of you drift gently into my mind.

They linger for moments then fade away

As dew on a sunny day,

Leaving a small and wistful smile in their wake.

The journey from heart and mind

And back again

In an instant and a lifetime.

Time to Go

I normally like to think things out

Give folks the benefit of the doubt

But there are times I have found

It's wisest not to hang around

When my stomach starts to churn

That's the time to leave, I've learned

So much better to trust my gut

Than be stabbed in the back or knocked on my butt

When things seem too good to be true

I watch my back and wallet too.

Three Meetings to Go

With just one step

On the wild side

I found myself

On a crazy ride.

Could have gotten off

But was having too much fun

Getting into trouble

And going on the run.

I'd beaten the odds.

I'd beaten them all.

It was somebody else

Who always took the fall.

Then one fateful day

I killed a man in Santa Fe.

I tried to make it out of town

But an angry mob chased me down.

Now just three more meetings

Before I'm done.

Between the Hangman and me

Is number one.

But it's the third I most fear

As the end of my life draws near.

Number two is with

The Undertaker.

Then I've got to

To face my Maker.

To My Beloved on Valentine's Day

We started as kids playing in the street

In basketball you were hard to beat

I loved when we played hide-and-seek at night

Using the glow of a big street light

Then we met years later at the house of a friend

When we started to talk, I knew it right then

That we'd be together for the rest of our lives

And someday you'd become my wife

Six months later, I was down on one knee

On a little bridge on a beautiful creek

Half a year later, we walked down the aisle

Thirteen months later, we had our first child

And though we had a lot of growing up to do

It wasn't long before we had child number two

And our blessings were soon doubled

As we had more good times than troubles

We made sure a girl was child number three

We had great times and some tough ones too

But always together we made it through

We never gave in and never gave up

We worked together and made our own luck

We've made a great love as we built our life

And I still bless the day you became my wife

To My Grandsons

With you I see the world

Through a child's eyes

Everything's a mystery

A wonderful surprise.

I'll teach you a thing or two

I've learned along the way

I know you'll be the kind of men

Who'll help the world each day.

To See How High They Can Fly

Sometimes words start forming in my head

And that can be a good place to start

But I'm happier with what I write

When words start flowing from my heart

For it's from there my spirit sings

And helps my words to have wings

Sends them soaring to the sky

To see how high they can fly

Transformation

May my last breath

At the end of my race

Be used to whisper "Wahoo!"

With a smile on my face.

May awesome wonder

Be reflected in my eyes

As my next adventure

Begins to materialize.

True Ones Stay

When times are bleak

Hope falls away

False friends leave

But true ones stay.

In darkest times

Shine bright the latter,

Show they're the ones

Who truly matter.

Truth Beckoned

Do I dare to heed its call?
Fought it for so long
Did all I could to stall
But I learned that I was wrong
When bigotry was all I knew
Safety was with my own kind
So I remained captive
To my own closed mind
Refused to let the light in
To my dark and dank cell
Suffocated in that prison
My own private kind of hell
The light of truth beckoned
Got too bright to ignore
I'd simply learned too much
To wear blinders anymore
I was done making excuses
Time to set myself free

From false beliefs and biases
That had blinded me
I pulled out my ignorance
Right down to its roots
Faced my fear to finally find
The beauty of my truth

Truth

When I want to learn the truth
About what I've seen or heard
I take the time to remind myself
Actions speak louder than words.

What Comes Next

The end of each day

Begins a new night sky

The end of a caterpillar

Begins a beautiful butterfly

So I look forward to what comes next

After the moment I die.

What Warms My Heart Cells

What wakes up my brain cells is a good thing.

From fantasy and laughter to caffeine's zing.

But what warms my heart cells is finding kindness anywhere,

To feel that great connection when seeing people

    show they care.

When No One Else Was

Thank you
To all who
Were there with love
When no one else was
Or would have been
Had you known me then.

Where Beauty's Found

Ugly is in the mind of the beholder.
The heart is where beauty's found.
Why focus on the ugly
When beauty is all around?

Where Do Dreams Go to Die?

Where do dreams go to die?
Could be an awful, terrible place.
But caterpillars become butterflies.
Drops of water become snowflakes.
Perhaps dreams are like that too
When they're crushed and all seems lost.
Maybe they become something new
Even better than what we'd sought.

Why?

When I say I'll be done in five minutes and she's waiting for me
She tells me I'm taking ten when it's only been three
But when she says she needs five minutes for her to be done
I'm still waiting and waiting when it's been thirty-one!

Why Stop at Lemonade?

"When life gives you lemons make lemonade."

We've all heard that worn-out phrase before

But why stop at making lemonade

When we can have a whole lemon smorgasbord?

We all get a lot of lemons in our lives from time to time

So it's good to know what to do with them for goodness' sake

I've learned a long list of goodies I can make with mine

From lemon meringue pie, cookies, bars, and cake

I can swap my lemons

For coconuts, pineapples, and limes

We'll add a little rum

And have a real fun time

I hope this poem is a good reminder

That there are no limits to what you can do

Or how much fun you can create

With all the lemons that life gives to you

Worthy

It took two bad lungs

And a broken heart

To finally tear

My world apart

Barely alive

In intensive care

Hoping friends would

Visit me there

Most were too busy

To visit at all

To send a card

Or bother to call

Barely able to breathe

Alone and in pain

I felt betrayed

And they were to blame

But the truth came suddenly

A cold and bitter wind

To have the love I wanted

I'd need to BE a better friend

I made a vow to the broken man

Who had 'til then been me

I'd get well and then become

The best friend I could be

I became one who could be counted on

No matter what the plight

From a shoulder to cry on

To help on a rainy night

Now life is so much better

I am truly blessed

For when it comes to friends

I have the very best

Yesterday's Heroes

Why are yesterday's heroes
Often quickly forgotten?
That mystery saddens me.
But what weighs on me more
Is how history's worst villains
Are remembered forever
For their sins and wars.

You Light Me Up!

You do so much more than satisfy
With your touch you electrify
You Light Me Up!
Lit up from the inside out!
Every part of me wants to shout
You Light Me Up!
Like fireworks exploding high
Brightening the whole night sky
You Light Me Up!
Your lightning flashes deep inside
My heart has nowhere else to hide
You Light Me Up!
Like the sun at noon
Or the glow of the moon
You Light Me Up!
You make every day brighter
And every night lighter
You Light Me Up!

You're a Beautiful Memory

Long after you've gone

Your memory brings

Hope in the deepest

Depths of despair

Beauty when ugly

Seems everywhere

Love to transform apathy

Wisdom to help my eyes to see

Light that shines through darkest days

Direction to help me find my way

Compassion of the warmest kind

Helps to ease my troubled mind

Frees my soul from tyranny

Your memory brings such gifts to me

Blessings I rely upon

To stay alive

Long after you've gone

About the Author

Russ lives with his wife in Campbell, California. They've been married since 1979 and have three children and three grandsons. In addition to enjoying his family and friends, and his dual passions for investing and writing, Russ loves to spend time in nature, especially near rivers and streams that run through giant redwood groves, and near beautiful beaches. He enjoys watching classic movies, reading, and tending to his small fern garden and redwood grove. Russ manages the investments of the wealth management firm he founded in 2003.

Russ's books can all be found on Amazon.com.
His Amazon Author Page can be found at
www.amazon.com/author/russtowne.

The titles of the books he has written or compiled, published, and released include:

Nonfiction

From the Heart of a Grateful Man

Reflections of a Grateful Man

Slices of Life—An anthology of the selected nonfiction stories of several writers.

Fiction

Palpable Imaginings—An anthology of fictional short stories by several writers in various genres

Touched—Short stories and flash fiction

Poetry

Tickletoe Tree Poetry

Heart Whispers—A powerful and touching anthology of the selected works of over twenty poets.

Books for Young Children

A Day in the Shade of a Tickletoe Tree

Tickletoe Tree Poetry

Purple Fox and the Heebie Jeebies

The Grumpadinkles

Zach and the Toad Who Rode a Bull

Misty Zebracorn

V. G. and Dexter Dufflebee

Ki-Gra's REALLY, REALLY BIG Day!

The Duck Who Flew Upside Down

Clyde and Friends

Clyde and Hoozy Whatzadingle

Clyde and I Help a Hippo to Fly

Rusty Bear and Thomas Too

Clyde and I

Russ has four blogs:

A Grateful Man (nonfiction uplifting posts)
http://russtowne.com

A Grateful Man's Poetry http://agratefulmanspoetry.com

Imaginings of a Grateful Man (fictional short stories)
http://imaginingsofagratefulman.com

Clyde and Friends (About writing children's stories)
http://clydeandfriends.com

Why Russ Writes

Russ hopes readers experience truth and kindness
in his writing, to remind everyone of the greatness and
goodness within themselves and others.

www.ingramcontent.com/pod-product-compliance
Lightning Source LLC
Chambersburg PA
CBHW051902090426
42811CB00003B/432